YOUNG AND OLD

Leo has just moved to live in a new area ... he has very few young neighbours ... he has difficulty making friends ... until he meets Gloria ... but her life is in danger ... can Leo save her?

RESCUING GLORIA

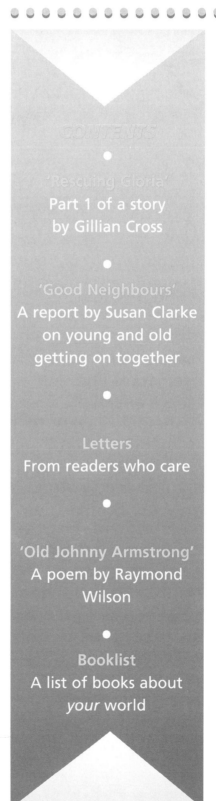

Cows would be *better*, thought Leo. *Or PIGS! There's no one decent living near here.* He glared through the front window of the new flat, and thought how he hated Mercy Street. How he hated the neat, sweet houses opposite with their perfect, tidy gardens. Five little ones in a terrace and a big one on the corner. The people in them were all OLD. Grannies and grandads. *Great*-grannies and great-*great*-grandads! He hadn't seen anyone under a hundred and fifty since they had moved in. He stamped angrily through the sitting room and glared at the view through his bedroom window instead. That was even worse. Even cows and pigs couldn't live in that jungle. Because his window was at the end of the block, it looked sideways, towards the big corner house next door. The house was empty, and its huge garden was a wild tangle of plants. There was no one there at *all!* Grannies or empty houses! Leo scowled at his reflection in the mirror.

Then his mum wandered into the bedroom, with baby Alice tucked under one arm and a table lamp in the other hand. 'Do you think we should put this in here? We seem to have so much *stuff*.'

Waving the lamp round vaguely, she suddenly caught sight of Leo's face and sighed.

'Cheer *up*, Leo. We've only been here three days, you know. Give it time. You'll meet plenty of people once school starts.'

'But that's six weeks!'
His mother frowned. 'Well, what about that girl downstairs? I'm sure she's about your age.'

'What girl?'

'In that flat with all the pot plants. Couldn't you make friends with her?'

'I – ' Leo wasn't sure how he felt about making friends with a strange girl. 'I might go and take a look.'

Slowly, still feeling sulky, he pulled on his best jacket and let himself out of the front door. Quietly, because he didn't want to get caught by someone old and boring.

Once he was out in Mercy Street, he could see what his mother meant by *that flat with all the pot plants*. One of the ground-floor flats looked as though it had a forest inside. Plants crowded the windowsill, spreading thick green leaves across the glass. They climbed up the sides of the window, hung down from the top and drooped across the middle. The girl was harder to spot because she was almost hidden by plants.

But she was there all right, behind the leaves, busy with a watering can. There was something brisk and business-like about her face and about the way she inspected each plant before she watered it.

Leo walked up and down a couple of times, grinning in her direction, but she didn't notice him. He even waved, but he might as well have been invisible.

Oh, that was *really* wonderful, wasn't it! At last he'd found someone his own age – and all she cared about was plants! His smile faded and he felt awkward and stupid.

Leo decided to go and explore the town. It was the holidays, after all, and people from the school must be hanging around somewhere.

With a last glance at the girl –

who was peering down at a weedy little plant in a yoghurt pot – he walked off up the road.

As he got to the corner, ready to turn into Grace Road, he heard a baby screaming, worse than Alice on a bad day. *I HATE this town!* he thought, for the millionth time. *There's only one thing worse than grannies, and that's BABIES. I'd like to run away to –*

But before he decided where to run to, he walked round the corner – and saw a crowd of boys, around his own age. They were standing by a lamp-post, about a hundred metres away, chatting and kicking a football about.

Leo stood still for a moment or two and looked at them.

They seemed OK. Especially the one in the middle, with the red hair and the grin. He strolled towards them, as slowly as he could, but they were busy with the ball and they didn't even notice him.

Until he came up to the lamp-post. Then, just as he reached it, the red-haired boy threw himself at the ball, in a wild tackle. He was flung backwards, by three or four of the others, and he landed hard on Leo's foot.

'Hey! Sorry! Are you OK?'

For a couple of seconds, he was actually grinning apologetically at Leo. Now was the moment to make friends! All Leo had to do was say – say –

But his mind was empty. He couldn't think of a thing to say. Not a question to ask, not a joke to make. And while he was dithering, the others yelled at the red-haired boy.

'Course he's OK. Let him alone, Kevin.'

'Think he's made of glass or something?'

Kevin turned away. Leo was furious with himself for missing a chance like that. They must be thinking he was a complete idiot!

He went on walking until he got to the end of Grace Road and went round the corner into the High Street. Then, when he was out of sight, he stopped beside a battered old Land Rover, to catch his breath. His heart thudded as if he had been running and he wanted to scream. What a fool he was! How was he *ever* going to get people to talk to him?

As he asked himself the question, he felt a sharp tug on the back of his jacket. For one, wild moment he thought the red-haired boy might have followed him. He whirled round – and found himself looking into a pretty face with two big eyes.

Square eyes.

There was a goat in the back of the Land Rover and it had stuck its head out and taken a mouthful of his jacket.

'Hey!' Leo said. '*Hey!*'

He pulled at the jacket, but not very hard because he didn't want to tear it. The goat stared at him, in a friendly way, and clamped its teeth even tighter.

'Let go!' Leo shouted. 'Come on, you crazy goat. Let go of my jacket!'

Delicately, the goat lifted its head, pulling the jacket. There was only one way to save it from being ripped, Leo realised. He would have to take it off. Feeling rather foolish, he began to slip his arms out of the sleeves.

There was a giggle behind him and two voices called, 'Harjinder! Harjinder!'

'Do you want any help?' said another voice. An older one that sounded friendly.

Leo looked round and saw a tall girl with long black plaits coming down the road towards him. She was carrying a heavy bag of shopping in each hand and two giggling little boys were running round her.

'Harjinder!' they shouted.

'The goat,' Leo said, feeling an idiot. 'It's got my jacket.'

He thought Harjinder would shriek with laughter, but she didn't seem a shrieking kind of person. She looked carefully at the goat and then she gave him a grin. Friendly and calm.

'Let's see if it likes this better than your jacket.'

She put her shopping down and took a paper bag full of carrots out of one of the carriers. Tipping the carrots on to the rest of the shopping she held out the paper bag.

For a second, the goat stared at her with its solemn, square eyes. Then, to Leo's amazement, it dropped his jacket and snatched at the paper bag.

'Hey, that's brilliant! What made you think of that?'

Harjinder picked up her shopping again. 'Didn't you know goats like paper?'

The bag was disappearing rapidly as the goat chewed. All Leo could do was stare.

'Why don't they get indigestion?' he said after a moment or two.

But there was no answer. Harjinder had solved his problem and gone. When he looked round, he saw her disappearing round the corner, talking busily to the two boys. He hadn't even said thank you.

Sadly, Leo scratched the lumpy top of the goat's head. 'You're the only person in this whole town who's got time for me, as far as I can see.'

As the goat swallowed the last of the paper bag, he thought how pretty it was. Its coat was a pale honey colour, and everything about it was delicate: its wispy beard, its spiky eyelashes and the fine white lines down each side of its nose.

Leo went on scratching gently, and wondered why it was easier to meet goats than people in this town.

Then a voice spoke behind him. A very thick gruff voice. 'Hey, Gloria, what are you up to? Chatting up strangers?'

Leo turned and saw a very, *very* old man coming out of the nearest building. He was older than any of the people in Mercy Street, with loose brown skin that wrinkled into a thousand creases.

Gloria the goat turned towards him, snuffling her nose into his hand as he got close. He pulled gently at one of her ears.

'I wasn't hurting her,' Leo said

quickly. 'Only talking to her.'

'I can tell that, boy. She likes you.' The old man took a chunk of cabbage out of his coat pocket. 'Give her this.'

Rather nervously, Leo took the cabbage and held it out. Gloria lunged forward to take a bite.

'That's it, girl,' the old man said. His voice crackled strangely. 'You have some fun while you can. You've only got another ten minutes or so.'

Leo looked at Gloria as she chewed. 'Why only ten minutes? What's going to happen then?'

Leo looked and saw that the building was a vet's. 'Is she ill?'

'She's got a bad case of motorways,' the old man said bitterly.

'Motorways?' For a second Leo wondered if it was a goat disease.

'They're building the new motorway slap-bang through my smallholding,' the old man said. 'No by-your-leave. No chance to refuse. They just sent me the money and told me I'd got to get out. Compulsory purchase, they call it.' He spat into the gutter.

'So why don't you buy somewhere else?' Leo said.

'With the money they gave me? Not a chance. I'm going to live with my son, in his flat in Coventry.'

'A flat.' Leo looked at Gloria. It was impossible to imagine her in a flat.

'That's it.' The old man nodded. 'I can't take her. But no one else will have her either. It was easy to give away my chickens, but who wants a goat?'

Leo looked at the vet's nameplate beside the door, 'So what's going to happen to her?'

'She's going to be put to sleep,' the old man said harshly. 'I've hung on as long as I could, but I'm leaving for Coventry in two hours and that's all I can do with her.'

'Put to sleep!' Leo looked at Gloria. 'But that's dreadful!'

'Course it's dreadful.' The old man unfastened the back of the

Land Rover. 'But what else can I do? Do you know a spare bit of ground where she can go and live?' He caught hold of the chain fixed to Gloria's collar and she jumped down on to the road.

'I –'

Suddenly, the words made a picture in Leo's head. The picture of the spare piece of ground that was overgrown and tangled. *Gloria could live in the wild garden next door. The one he could see from his bedroom window.*

Quickly he grabbed her chain. 'Don't go in there. I do know a place. I've got somewhere she can live!'

The old man looked at him very hard. 'Where?'

'It's –' Leo didn't want to explain exactly. 'It's where I live.'

Next... Leo has to get the goat to her new home but she has other ideas!

GOOD
Neighbours...

*I*t is sometimes claimed that young people and old people don't get on very well.

This is not true in one Yorkshire community, where elderly residents are finding that their lives are being made brighter by local children.

Class 6 of Butly Junior School are running a 'Good Neighbours' scheme, which is improving relationships with elderly people living in nearby bungalows.

The children came up with the idea themselves after complaints that thoughtless children were being noisy and dropping litter on their way to and from school.

This upset Sarah Ibison and her friends so much that they decided to go and clear up the mess, even though they hadn't dropped it! They got talking to some of the residents and things developed from there.

'We asked our teacher if we could visit some of the old people during our dinner hours,' Sarah told me.

'Soon the rest of the class heard and wanted to be involved. Our teacher helped us to contact more people and to arrange visits. Now the whole class are helping our older neighbours in lots of ways.'

Many of the old people find looking after their small gardens difficult. The children help by doing jobs such as weeding and planting bulbs. They go on errands to the local shops and even help with housework.

Susan Clarke has been finding out about an exciting link between children at a Yorkshire school and old people who live close by.

It isn't all work. Old and young have fun together. One of those involved, seventy-four-year-old Mrs Vera Chadwick, smiled as she told us:

'Sometimes we all sing. I've taught the children some of the songs I used to enjoy when I was young. At Christmas they bought me a Christmas tree, decorations, mince pies and a present. We enjoy talking to the young people and learning about their lives.'

Eleven-year-old Mark Brough described what the children gain:
'We talk about what life was like when they were younger and what they got up to in the old days. They make us tea and give us biscuits.'

The children have recently come up with a new 'treat' for their older friends. They take their pets on the visits too!

The headteacher of Butly Juniors, Mrs Pauline Bell, is proud of the scheme. *'This school's relationship with our neighbours is very important. We are lucky to have the senior citizens living close by. Everyone involved is developing increased understanding, and the children and the elderly feel themselves to be part of a larger, caring, considerate community.'*

If the splendid efforts of these Yorkshire youngsters impress *you* why not set up your own 'Good Neighbours' scheme?

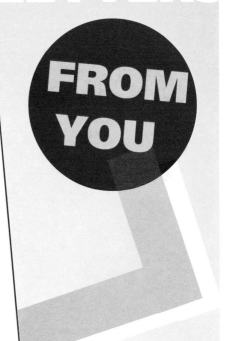

Dear Editor,

May I express my pleasure on reading about the 'Good Neighbours' scheme. I would like to suggest ways in which it might be extended.

The police might be pleased to set up a Home/School Watch. The old people would keep an eye on the school at night, weekends and during holidays. In return the children would keep an eye on the homes of the old people. This might reduce vandalism and the risk of break-ins.

The children are obviously respecting and valuing the Senior Citizens as members of the community and as friends.

It's really good to read about people helping others. Such unselfishness deserves praise and encouragement. The old people feel less lonely, the young more useful.

Yours sincerely,
Jane Cale
Weymouth, Dorset

Dear Sir,

I write to complain about the idea of old people being visited by children. There are several reasons why I disagree.

1. It's a lot of work for the old people. They shouldn't be expected to make tea for visitors.

2. The idea that children bring their pets to visit the elderly is silly. Animals are often dirty and can be a cause of bad health. Dogs can bring hair and mess into the homes and people may be allergic to them, causing asthma.

3. There is a danger that the children are doing so many jobs that they are taken advantage of. The children deserve a rest at lunchtime.

Yours sincerely,
Martin Skinner
Stanmore, Middlesex

OLD JOHNNY ARMSTRONG

*A poem to think about...
Health, memories, friends and
visitors are just some of the
things which are important to
old people. Raymond
Wilson considers such
things in this poem.*

Old Johnny Armstrong's eighty or more
And he humps like a question-mark
Over two gnarled sticks as he shuffles
and picks
His slow way to Benwell Park.

He's lived in Benwell his whole life
long
And remembers how street-
lights came,
And how once on a time they
laid a tram-line,
Then years later dug up the
same!

Now he's got to take a lift to his
flat,
Up where the tall winds blow
Round a Council Block that rears like a
rock
From seas of swirled traffic below.

Old Johnny Armstrong lives out his life
In his cell on the seventeenth floor,
And it's seldom a neighbour will do
him a favour
Or anyone knock at his door.

With his poor hands
knotted with rheumatism
And his poor back doubled
in pain,
Why, day after day, should
he pick his slow way
To Benwell Park yet again? –

O the wind in park trees is
the self-same wind
That first blew on a village
child
When life freshly unfurled in
a green, lost world
And his straight limbs ran
wild.

BOOKLIST: *YOUR WORLD*

Our readers have read them and they recommend them! Go to your bookshop or library and ENJOY them!

'GREEN ISSUES'

Shades of Green
(Redfox) £3.50
Lots of poems which recognise that we cannot survive without nature. Full of inspiration, hope and surprises!

Rescue Mission – Planet Earth
(Kingfisher) £6.99
Children from all over the world wrote and illustrated this book. A chance for you to join their mission to rescue our world from environmental disaster.

HISTORY

Horrible Histories
(Scholastic) £2.99
With titles like 'The Awesome Egyptians', 'The Rotten Romans' and 'The Terrible Tudors', this series takes a very different and very funny view of history.

JUST FOR FUN

Fast Tricks to Amaze your Friends
(Headway) £2.99
The official book of the TV series Learn how to make a computer out of a matchbox, balance a spoon on your nose, read someone's mind! Really useful!

SCIENCE AND TECHNOLOGY

Newsround Book of Space
(BBC) £4.99
Where does space begin? What do scientists think of UFOs? Will people ever live in space? These and other questions are answered in this exciting book from the TV team.

Bio Facts
(Oxford) £3.99
Want to know about the human body? Animals? Plants? This detailed book provides accurate scientific facts at your fingertips.

How to Survive in the Jungle
(Simon and Schuster) £6.99
Stunning illustrations and an informed text. You'll be totally involved in the ecology of jungle life.

I Spy Wild Flowers
(Michelin) £1.25
One of a series. Challenges you to look at the world. How many can you spot? Good value and good illustrations.

CONTENTS

Name _____

INTRODUCTION FOR THE PARENT

KEY STAGE 2 NATIONAL TESTS

From 1995, all pupils in Year 6 (those aged between 10 and 11) will take National Key Stage 2 (KS2) Tests in the three core subjects: Science, Mathematics and English. The results of these tests will be reported to parents and eventually published.

The KS2 Test results should not be used to determine which secondary school your child will attend. However, they will be available to all secondary schools and they may well be used to place your child into the appropriate teaching group. Good test results, together with a positive report from the primary school, will ensure your child is placed in a higher group. In turn, this means your child will study the higher levels of the Key Stage 3 curriculum.

HOW THIS SERIES WILL HELP YOUR CHILD

This series aims to:

- Give your child plenty of practice in the types of question he or she will face in the KS2 test

- Provide answers and a mark scheme to allow you to check how your child has done

- Offer advice which will help to improve skills and answers

- Help you to estimate at which level of the National Curriculum your child is working.

The work attempted at KS2 is demanding. But these books will help you to become involved in your child's studying and offer real help in reaching the best possible level of attainment.

ENGLISH FOR KS2

At the heart of the National Curriculum for English are the Programmes of Study for Speaking and Listening, Reading and Writing.

Your child's achievements in these areas are set against levels of attainment described in the Attainment Targets (ATs). The first AT, Speaking and Listening, is assessed only by the teacher in the classroom, not in the written KS2 tests. The other ATs are:

- AT2: Reading

- AT3: Writing

- ATs 4 and 5 which are concerned with Spelling and Handwriting.

The National Curriculum divides each subject into a number of levels. It is reasonable to expect that, by the end of KS2, most children should be between Levels 3 and 5. Some children might reach Level 6, and this should be recognised as an excellent result.

A PARENT'S GUIDE TO USING THIS BOOK

The questions in this book allow children to show some of their abilities as readers (pages 2–11), writers (pages 12–18) and spellers and handwriters (pages 19–21).

Together the tests enable a range of National Curriculum levels, between 2 and 6, to be gained. You will find details of the elements of the Programmes of Study being assessed on pages 22 (reading), 29 (writing) and 45 (spelling and handwriting).

SIMULATING TEST CONDITIONS

Allow your child to do these three tests on separate occasions. Set the reading test first, preferably on a different day from the other two. Allow a break (for example, lunchtime) between the writing test and the spelling and handwriting test.

Detailed requirements of timings and the way to approach each test can be found on page 1 (The Reading Test), page 12 (The Writing Test) and page 19 (The Spelling and Handwriting Test). Provide a clock, enabling your child to complete the starting and finishing times at the beginning of the tests.

Remind your child of the need to concentrate but to minimise tension – encourage him or her to *enjoy* these tests.

MARKING THE ANSWERS

Answers to the reading test are on pages 23–27. Boxes in the margins of the question section show the marks available for each question, enabling you to note the number of marks your child scores. The totals box for reading is on page 11.

Judgements about your child's performance in the writing test are informed by pages 30–41. Detailed information about marking the spelling and handwriting test appears on pages 46 and 49.

Scores from these different components are brought together on pages 51–52, enabling you to place your child's overall performance in these tests against National Curriculum levels.

Most pupils working well at the age of 11 will be in the Levels 3–5 range. If your child is in this range there is nothing to worry about. Some children will achieve Level 6, and if your child does this it is very good. Although the National Curriculum levels go beyond 6 it is not possible to achieve higher levels at the age of 11 as this would require the child to have been taught Key Stages 3 and 4 Programmes of Study.

A PARENT'S GUIDE TO THE READING TEST

To answer the questions in the reading test your child must first read the magazine 'Young and Old' which follows page 52 of this booklet. Detatch it carefully and staple or clip it together. Now read through these instructions and the Information for the Parent on page 22. Make sure you are thoroughly familiar with what your child will be working on.

Introduce your child to the magazine and briefly summarise the four sections of writing in it.

Now ask your child to turn to where the story 'Rescuing Gloria' begins on page 1 of the magazine. Read out the short instructions on page 2 of this book and explain that he or she has 20 minutes to read through the magazine and after this will have to answer questions about it.

Allow your child 20 minutes to read quietly, and fairly quickly. If your child finishes the story, he or she should carry on through the magazine. When the 20 minutes have elapsed, ask your child to stop reading. Reassure him or her that there is no need to worry if he or she has not finished reading everything in the magazine.

Your child needs the magazine and the reading test section (pages 3–11) as he or she works through the test.

Now read aloud the example question on page 2 with your child and help him or her to answer it correctly.

In your own words describe how your child should work through the test, making sure to include these points:

• Wherever the pencil symbol appears an answer must be written.

• If a question is too hard, your child should go on to the next one.

• He or she may look at the magazine as often as needed when answering the questions.

• After finishing a page he or she should turn over to a new page without waiting to be told.

• Marks will not be given for spelling, handwriting, punctuation or grammar in this part of the English test.

• There are 50 minutes to complete this test.

Note the starting time in the appropriate place on page 3. When 50 minutes have elapsed ask your child to stop. Note the finishing time in the appropriate place.

When you have completed the marking add up the marks to give a Reading Test Total, and enter this in the box provided on page 11. You will need this total mark when finding your child's KS2 level on page 51.

READING

INSTRUCTIONS

The questions in this section are about the contents of your magazine: the story, the information piece about 'Good Neighbours', the poem and the booklist.

Your parent will explain how you are to do the first task by going through the following example with you.

As your parent reads the example aloud you will see four possible answers. In each case choose the best word, or group of words, to fit the passage and put a ring round it.

You may look at the magazine as often as you wish when you are answering the questions.

GOOD LUCK!

EXAMPLE

The title of this magazine is

Young and Old   Getting Together   Friends   Being Alone

and the story is about a goat called:

George   Gloria   Gina   Gordon

Now please wait until your parent tells you to start work on page 3 in the same way.

When you have finished page 3 you should turn over the page and carry on working through to the end of the reading section of this book (page 11).

READING

ABOUT THE STORY Questions 1–9

Start [　　　　]
Finish [　　　　]

1. At the start of the story Leo glared through the

door　　　　(window)　　　　mirror　　　　mist .

□ 1

2. He was unhappy, he wished he lived near

rats and
mice　　　(cows and
pigs)　　　cats and
dogs　　　ducks and
geese .

□ 1

3. Leo let himself out of the house quietly because he didn't want to

meet somone
his own age　　wake baby
Alice　　spot the girl
in the flat　　(get caught by
someone old) .

□ 1

4. Leo spent time outside the window where a girl was watering plants because he

(wanted her
to notice him)　　already
knew her　　liked
nature　　thought she
was lonely .

□ 1

5. How did the red-haired boy feel about bumping into Leo?

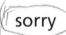
glad　　　　frightened　　　　(sorry)　　　　angry .

□ 1

6. When Leo met Harjinder he thought she seemed

(friendly)　　bad-mannered　　cheeky　　unhelpful .

□ 1

7. When the goat let go of his jacket Leo was

(disappointed) ✗　　amazed　　unhappy　　sad .

□ 1

8. The old man was getting rid of Gloria because

he was fed
up with her　　(she was
ill) ✗　　he was
losing his land　　Leo liked
her　　.

but Leo knew a place where she could live!

□ 1

3

AT2
Level 3-6

WHAT HAPPENS IN THE STORY?

9. Here are some of the events that have happened in the story so far. Put all these events in the right order by numbering each line. The first event has been numbered for you.

___4___ stops by a Land Rover

___7___ meets the old man who owns Gloria

___3___ meets boys playing football

___1___ Leo moves to a new home

___6___ Harjinder rescues Leo

___2___ spots the girl watering plants

___5___ a goat tugs Leo's jacket

2

ABOUT THE CHARACTERS   Questions 10–16

10. Why does Leo hate the houses in Mercy Street?

Leo hated Mercy Street because the people living there were grannies and grand dads.

1

1

11. Leo stopped beside a battered old Land Rover. Why did he want to scream?

He wanted to scream because he felt angry with himself for not making friends with the red head boy.

1

1

4

12. Why did Leo feel it was easier to meet goats than people in the town?

every one he met they were hard to speak to.

2

2

13. Why did Leo think that the man he talked to was very, *very* old?

He thought the was old because the man had loose brown skin that wrinkled.

1

1

14. Why can the old man tell that Gloria likes Leo?

He can tell gloria likes him because when leo gave her the cabbage she jumped to the cabbage.

✗

2

15. Why doesn't Leo want to explain exactly where he lives?

Leo did'nt what explain exactly because he was rushing.

✗

2

16. In this episode we read about Leo and other people including the girl watering plants, the footballing boy, Harjinder who gets his coat back, the old man who owned Gloria, and others. He is going to meet one of these people in the next episode of the story.

Who do you think it is? I think it the red head boy

a. Explain why you think it is this person.

It is this person because they had bumbed into each other before.

!

1

b. Write a possible heading for the next episode of Leo's story.

I think he starts to getting freinds.

1

HOW THE STORY IS WRITTEN   Questions 17–21

17. In the first paragraph of the story the writer makes it clear that Leo is not happy about moving to the new flat.

✎ Find five different words which she uses to show his feelings.

(glared)   (hated)   (Old people)

(angrily)   (grannies and grandads)

18. The writer gives a vivid picture of the flat with all the pot plants.

✎ Find three words which describe this vegetation.

(plants)   (girl)   (pot)

19. The old man says that Gloria has 'got a bad case of the motorways'.

✎ Explain what he means.

_____

_____

_____

20. Gloria's owner tells Leo that the goat is going to be put to sleep.

What one word does the writer use to show the old man's anger and bitterness?

✎ (bitterly)

21. In this part of the story Leo has faced a number of situations which have caused him problems.

Margin marks:

2
2

1

1

1

Letts

AT2
Level 3-6

List as many as you can here.

PROBLEMS FACING LEO

Leo's problems were that he hated the street and that he missed a chance of making freinds.

2

5

YOUR OPINION Questions 22–23

22. Would you be interested in reading the rest of this story?

Yes ( ) No (No)

Say what you liked or did not like about the part you have read so far.

I liked the bit when he wanted to scream.

3

23. You have read only the first part of Leo's story.

What do you think that the rest of the story might be about?

Why do you think so?

I think the story will turn out to be that he makes freinds.

2

2

20/36

ABOUT THE ARTICLE   Questions 1–4

1. Write down **THREE** things which the children do to help the old people.

The children helped by cleaning up the mess and by They got talking to the residents and by visingting the older

2. How did Sarah and her friends first meet their elderly neighbours?

By runing a neighbours scheme.

3. When we read the article we can guess the reporter's opinion about the 'Good Neighbours' scheme. What is her opinion?

_____

_____

_____

4. Write out **ONE** sentence or phrase that shows what she thinks about their work.

_____

_____

THE OPINIONS OF THE LETTER WRITERS
Questions 1–4

5. Both Martin and Jane wrote a P.S. at the end of their letters but these were not printed in the magazine. Which one wrote:

P.S. I hope the excellent links between the generations will continue when the children go to High School.

Jane

Marks column:
1
1
1

1

1

2

1

P.S. Isn't school about learning about Maths, Science and English, rather than visiting the elderly?

(Martin)

1

1

6. Look again at Martin's points. He is saying that pets are often dirty and can cause bad health.

a. In what way does he think that they can be *dirty*?

He thinks they can be often dirty because of the bad health.

1

1

b. In what way does Martin think that they could be bad for people's health?

He think that the old people could be allergic to them that can cause them asma.

1

1

7a. Look again at the letter from Jane. Who does she think will welcome her School/Home Watch plan?

She thinks that the police will welcome her watch plan.

1

1

b. Why might the scheme be welcome?

1

8. Which letter do you agree with? Jane's or Martin's? Perhaps you have a different point of view. Write down what *you* think about the article and say why.

I agree with Janes letter because she not complaining like saying the Animals will make some old people allergic she pointing out the facts about how nice it is.

2

2

9

READING

ABOUT THE POEM   Questions 1–5

1. Why is Johnny Armstrong described as being like a question mark?

He is ~~nown as a~~ described as being like a question mark because he humps like to gnarled sticks.

1

2. How has Benwell changed during Johnny's life?

He remembers how street light came and how once on a time they laid a tram line.

1

3. In verse four, what does the poet's choice of the word 'cell' tell you about Johnny's life?

That old Jhonny Amstrong lives out his life on the Daventeenth Floor And seldom a neighbour will do him a favour our anymore knock at his door

1

4. Why, do you think, does Johnny go to the park day after day?

He remembers the wind in park trees is the selfsame wind That first blew on a village child.

2

5. What are your feelings about Johnny Armstrong's life, now that he is eighty or more?

~~He remembers~~ the wind I feel really sorry. That is just how some old people are treated.

2

10

Letts

AT2
Level 3-6

USING THE BOOKLIST

1. Look at page 12 of your magazine.

Which book would you choose for the following? The first one has been done for you.

Information about your own body?

Bio Facts

Poetry about the natural world?

Shades of green

| 1 |
| 1 |

Information about UFOs?

Newsround Book of Space

| 1 |
| 1 |

Survival in the jungle?

How to Survive in the Jungle

| 1 |
| 1 |

An amusing view of life in Ancient Egypt?

Horrible Histories The Awesome Egyptians

| 1 |
| 1 |

	Reading Test Score	
'Rescuing Gloria'	20	36
'Good Neighbours'	8	14
'Old Johnny Armstrong'	7	7
Booklist	4	4
READING TEST TOTAL	39	61

A PARENT'S GUIDE TO THE WRITING TEST

Explain to your child that he or she is going to write a story or description on his or her own and within a time limit. Before doing this there will be some time to plan it, preparing some notes which he or she can refer to during the writing session. Emphasise that he or she is writing a short story or a brief episode from a story or a description, not a long chapter from a novel.

Allow five or ten minutes to talk with your child about interesting short stories or descriptions which he or she may have read or written recently. You may wish to focus on the extract from 'Rescuing Gloria' and, for descriptive writing, 'Old Johnny Armstrong'. This discussion should revise your child's awareness of:

IN A STORY

• *beginning* in a way that captures the reader's attention;

• the importance of initiating the *action* and setting the *plot* in motion quickly in a short story;

• a manageable number of *characters* who can be developed using comments, description and dialogue (conversation);

• *continuing* in a way that makes the reader interested in what happens next;

• bringing the short story to a convincing conclusion.

IN A DESCRIPTION

• gaining and keeping the reader's attention;

• considering different aspects of the subject of the description;

• using a range of interesting descriptive vocabulary;

• making interesting comparisons;

• finishing the description in an interesting way.

Now read the general instructions on page 13 to your child. Go through the starting points together. Your child will choose the title which he or she thinks will make the best short story. Make sure your child understands how to plan the story, using the planning sheets on pages 15 and 16 or his or her own method of planning. Allow 15 minutes planning time for your child to think about what to write and to plan his or her story or description. If your child needs less planning time he or she can begin to write when ready.

Writing sheets are provided in this book on pages 17 and 18. Provide more A4 paper for your child if necessary. Allow 45 minutes for writing time. Enter the starting and finishing times in the appropriate places on page 17.

When you have finished the marking add up the marks to give a Writing Test Total and enter this in the box provided on page 18. You will need this total mark when finding your child's KS2 level on page 51.

WRITING

INSTRUCTIONS

Here are some starting points for writing and two planning sheets to help you organise your ideas.

Your parent will go through each one of the starting points with you, and explain how to use the space for planning your writing before you start.

You will have 15 minutes in which to think about what to write and to jot down your ideas.

You will then have 45 minutes to complete your writing.

Choose **ONE** starting point. Then use the appropriate planning sheet on page 15 or 16 to help plan your writing.

STARTING POINTS

1. **Making friends**

   Leo had moved to a new home and didn't know how to get people to talk to him.

   Imagine you go to live somewhere new where you don't know anyone.

   Write a short story about what happens.

2. **Future life**
   Imagine what your life will be like in the year 2050. You will be about seventy years old! Much may have happened to yourself and in the world about you.

   Write a short story about your life. You may wish to tell your reader about:

- what the world is like in the middle of the next century;

- your own way of life and family;

- your feelings at this time in your life.

3. **Story starters**

   Choose **ONE** of these for your story.

   EITHER:

   Write a short story with the title 'Animal Rescue'.

   OR:

   Write a short story which opens with this sentence:

   The house was empty, the mysterious garden a wild tangle inviting exploration.

4. **An interesting old person**

   The story and the poem both feature interesting old people.

   EITHER:

   Think of an older person known to yourself, for example a grandparent;

   OR:

   Make up an old person, using your knowledge of the lives of older people.

   Write a description of this person and his or her way of life.
   Have you chosen **ONE** of the starting points? Now, make a note of some of your ideas. Jot them down on a piece of paper, or turn over and use one of the planning sheets.

PLANNING SHEET (short story)

Which title have you chosen to write about?

Life in the future

Setting

London   Highbury   Same Buildings

no hole in the ozone layer Little crème

Characters (e.g. Who are they? What are they like?)

King william and me. Kw open person
Describe clothes - yellow woolly jumper Saying NoRWICH

What makes the story begin?

I was at a Football match
it was norwich vs Liverpool I was there
when he was getting a **What happens next?** with two freinds
burger I bumped into him. I got a Coke it spilt on him.
I said sorry + got out some tissues to dry him. He
invited me to sit in the spare seat next to him.

How will your story end? Who Won game
We really got on well and so he   What he said about it.
invited me to his birthday party. Spend lots of time
together at parties. going with him on trips in England + Abroad
Now we are best friends. He arranged for me to have a
house very near Buckingham Palace so I
Shared it with Ibukun
and he helped meking too

PLANNING SHEET (personal description)

THE OLDER PERSON

His or her appearance	His or her life in the past
His or her life now	**His or her character**

WRITING

_____

_____

_____

_____

_____

_____

_____

_____

_____

_____

_____

_____

_____

_____

_____

_____

_____

Ask for more paper if you need it.

	Writing Test Score
Purpose and Organisation	
Grammar	
Style	
WRITING TEST TOTAL	

A PARENT'S GUIDE TO THE SPELLING AND HANDWRITING TEST

SPELLING

This spelling test is likely to take 15 minutes.

In this test you will read the text of a story out loud to your child twice. Read it through the first time without stopping. Then read it aloud a second time, pausing in the appropriate places to allow your child to insert the missing words in his or her version of the story. The full text for your use is on page 46 and you can detach it if you wish. The words printed in bold italics are the words your child will have to spell. Your child's version of the story is on pages 20–21, with lines to complete in place of these words.

Encourage your child to make his or her best attempt at spelling even unfamiliar words. Allow sufficient time for each missing word to be written.

Read aloud the following instructions to your child. Adapt them or repeat them as you judge necessary.

• *I am going to read out a story called 'Through Space in Eternity'. I will read it twice.*

• *You will follow your version, which has words missing.*

• *Follow as I read through the passage for the first time. Don't write anything at this stage. I will then read it out again, giving you time to write the missing words in the gaps.*

Before the second reading tell your child:

• *I will now read the passage to you again.*

• *When you come to a gap wait for me to tell you the word and then write it in the space.*

• *If you are not sure how to spell it just have a go and write the letters you think are correct.*

Enter the starting and finishing times in the appropriate places.

Enter the score in the box provided on page 21. You will need this score when finding your child's KS2 level on page 51.

HANDWRITING

Allow five minutes for the handwriting test, which is on page 21.

In this test your child is asked to copy a few lines of the spelling test passage. Encourage him or her to do the best he or she can, but not to be too tense or to try too hard.

Enter the starting and finishing times in the appropriate places.

Enter the score in the box provided on page 21. You will need this score when finding your child's KS2 level on page 51.

SPELLING AND HANDWRITING

Start	6·05
Finish	6·20

Through Space in 'Eternity'

All around the Earth people ___looked___ on as

the ___time___ rapidly ___approached___

for the launch of United Nations' deep space craft *Eternity*.

Their minds were ___Concentrating___ on a billion virtual

___reality___ sets. The ___power___ of many lasers

___illuminated___ the launch site, cutting the African

night; tension was mounting inside the ___Command___

centre. The plan was to explore space in the remote control

craft, seeking some ___planet___ on which human

life could be established.

Why was this voyage taking place? By the year 2050 A.D.

Earth had become even more crowded. The population

multiplied and consumed at an ever-increasing rate. Human

selfishness had destroyed ___Nature___, now

humanity itself was threatened. It ___appeared___ that

nothing could prevent an environmental disaster.

The ___Capacity___ of the deep space craft was limited.

From a million volunteers from all over the ___World___

only one hundred were chosen. Life on a new planet would

be difficult. Tolerance, intelligence and _Confidence_

were particularly important qualities.

The journey they faced was long. Medical science knew

how to _Freeze_ them, injections of _gold_

would stop bones from _Crumbling_, artificial

material replaced blood.

Many dangers lay ahead. Barring _accidents_,

the travellers would reach their destination in 2150 A.D.,

having _slept_ for a century!

14	
1	
15	16
1	1
17	
1	
18	
1	
19	
1	
20	
1	

Spelling Score

18/20

Using your best joined-up writing, copy this last section on the
lines provided.

**Who could say how successful their journey might be? Could
this brave mission find a place for the human race, somewhere
deep in space?**

Who Could Say how Successful their journey might be? Could this brave mission find a place for the human race, Somewhere deep in Space? Some-where

Handwriting
Score

6

READING TEST ANSWERS

INFORMATION FOR THE PARENT – Reading at KS2: AT2

Effective teaching and learning at KS2 will have taken place when planned from the Programmes of Study for English and implemented in classrooms where talk, reading and writing are integrated. A wide variety of evidence about your child as a reader is available to his or her teacher; no test can identify and give a level to *any* reader's full range of achievements.

The KS2 reading test focuses on several elements from the Programmes of Study. It is designed to gather evidence about a child's ability to:

- read, understand and respond to a range of writing;

- understand and write about plot, setting, character and ideas in fiction;

- look at a text for details about character or action in order to draw conclusions, predict and make judgements;

- develop and express his or her own views and preferences, referring to details from a text to support his or her responses;

- use inference, deduction and previous reading experience to find and appreciate meanings beyond the literal;

- appreciate imaginative use of English and the effect of a writer's choice of words and phrases on the reader;

- select appropriate reference books;

- skim read;

- retrieve information.

NOTE TO PARENT

Before you mark your child's responses to the reading test do re-read the magazine. This will help you to clarify the information in the marking scheme and help you to judge the appropriateness of your child's answers. Different children will have different ways of wording the correct answer. Focus on the content of an answer, judging whether your child 'had the right idea'.

Insert the mark gained for each answer in the box adjoining the question on the outside of each page of the reading test. Make sure the mark you record is equal to or less than the mark(s) available for that question.

PAGE 3 SECTION 1: 'Rescuing Gloria'

Award one mark for each correct choice.

1. window	1 mark
2. cows and pigs	1 mark
3. get caught by someone old	1 mark
4. wanted her to notice him	1 mark
5. sorry	1 mark
6. friendly	1 mark
7. amazed	1 mark
8. he was losing his land	1 mark

NOTE TO PARENT

If your child has made no mark, or has circled two or more responses, no score is given. If he or she has underlined, ticked or indicated his or her choice in another way, then score the responses as indicated above.

9. The correct order is as follows:

4   stops by a Land Rover
7   meets the old man who owns Gloria
3   meets boys playing football
1   Leo moves to a new home
5   a goat tugs Leo's jacket
2   spots the girl watering plants
6   Harjinder rescues Leo

Award one mark for getting the start and end points correct (that is, getting 2 and 7 in the right place).

Award two marks for correctly ordering all stages.   2 marks

10. Accept any answer which refers to
                    the old people   1 mark

11. Accept any answer which refers to
                    getting people to talk to him.   1 mark

12. Award one mark for answers which indicate that
                    he has met the goat and made friends with it.

Award two marks for responses which indicate that
he has so far failed to get to know any people.   2 marks

23

13. Award one mark for any answers which refer to
his loose brown skin, wrinkled into a thousand creases.   1 mark

14. Award one mark for answers such as
He was being kind to her.

Award *another* mark if appropriate evidence is also provided, e.g.
Leo talking to the goat/scratching her ears
Gloria turning towards Leo, snuffling her nose into his hand
Leo pulling gently at one of her ears.
2 marks

15. Award one mark for any answer which refers to
living in a flat.

Award two marks for answers which give extra information, e.g.
the old garden not being part of his house
not having asked his parents.
2 marks

16. Do not score the response to the first question – about which character will return in the next episode.

a. Award one mark for any reasonable explanation supporting the prediction, e.g.
(the girl watering plants) because she is his age or *she lives near to him*
(Kevin, the footballing boy) because he seems O.K.
(Harjinder) because she seemed friendly or *she knows about goats.*
1 mark

b. Accept answers which follow on from the previous responses (to this question) and/or use information about the next episode, e.g.
getting the goat to her new home
the other ideas the goat has.

Do not accept answers which simply repeat word for word the information about the next episode.

1 mark

17. Award one mark if three words from the following list are given. Award a second mark if four or five appropriate words are given:
glared   hated   stamped   angrily   scowled   worse.   2 marks

18. Award 1 mark if three words from this list are given:
forest   crowded   spreading   thick   green   leaves
climbed   hung   drooped   hidden.   1 mark

19. Award one mark if the explanation shows understanding that the building of a motorway has led to the old man leaving his home, meaning that there is nowhere for Gloria to live.
1 mark

20. Award one mark for
harshly.   1 mark

21. Award one mark for reference to the following, up to a maximum of five marks:
moving to a new home
old people as neighbours
knowing no-one

failing to gain the attention of the plant watering girl
his baby sister
failing to befriend the footballing boys
Gloria grabbing his jacket
Harjinder disappearing
the threat of Gloria being 'put to sleep'
the need to give Gloria a home.

5 marks

22. Accept either YES or NO, but do not give a score for either response.

Score the reasons given as follows:
Award one mark for simplistic reasons, e.g.
It was good/it was boring.

Award two marks for a slightly more elaborate answer, possibly involving references to the texts or personal preferences, e.g.
I liked/did not like the way it was written.
I liked it when the goat grabbed Leo.

Award three marks for a well justified answer revealing close reference to the text, e.g.
I thought it was slow moving and more should have happened.
I thought the story told me about people's feelings.
I felt sorry for Leo/Gloria and hoped things would get better for him/her.
I thought that a lot had happened already.
I wanted to know what would happen to Gloria.
I thought the characters and situations were like real life.

3 marks

23. Award one mark to answers which make an acceptable prediction about the rest of the story and two marks to those that accompany the prediction with a sensible explanation.

Acceptable predictions include:
making friends
giving Gloria a good home/looking after her
changing attitude to old people.

Do not accept answers which refer only to *getting* the goat *to* her new home as these relate only to the next episode.

2 marks

Total 36 marks

PAGE 8 SECTION 2: 'Good Neighbours'

1. Award one mark (up to three) for any of the following:

looking after gardens
run errands
housework.

3 marks

2. Award one mark for answers which refer to cleaning up the litter/mess.

1 mark

3. Award one mark for simple answers, e.g.
She thinks it's a good idea.

Award two marks for expanded ideas, e.g.

> She thinks it's good for the old people to feel cared for and
> for the children to be understanding.

Note: Other reasons from the article are valid.   2 marks

4. Award one mark for any quotation from the text which reveals the positive opinions. Positive answers include:

> ... their lives being made brighter ...
> ... improving relationships ...
> Old and young have fun together.
> ... the splendid efforts of these Yorkshire youngsters ...

Check that the response is an actual quotation from the text.
                                                                                1 mark

PAGE 8 LETTERS

5. Award one mark if **BOTH** parts of the question are answered correctly:

> 'I hope the excellent links between the generations will
> continue when the children go to High School' – Jane

> 'Isn't school about learning about Maths,
> Science and English, rather than visiting the elderly?' – Martin
                                                                                1 mark

6a. Award one mark for answers which refer to
> *hair* and *mud*.
                                                                                1 mark

b. Award one mark for answers which make reference to all or any of the following:
> *hair   allergies   asthma*.
                                                                                1 mark

7a. Award one mark for the police.
                                                                                1 mark

b. Award one mark for any or all of these words:
> *pleasure   respecting   valuing   friends   good to read*
> *helping others   unselfish   praise and encouragement*.
                                                                                1 mark

8. Award one mark for answers which contain elements of a personal response, although justification from the text may be weak, e.g.
> 'I agree with Jane – it's a good scheme.'

Award two marks for answers revealing a grasp of the points and a personal response justified from the text, e.g.
> 'I agree with the article. People of different ages should get on
> with each other. Young and old are gaining. The old are helped and
> get company, the young are learning from the old.'

Do not accept answers which do not express a personal view or fail to refer intelligently to the text, e.g.
> 'Jane's because she's right.'
                                                                                2 marks

TOTAL 14 marks

PAGE 10 SECTION 3: 'Old Johnny Armstrong'

1. Award one mark for answers which refer in any way to his physical condition/the shape of his body.

1 mark

2. Award one mark for answers which refer to any of the following:

> *street lights*
> *trams*
> *traffic*
> *blocks of flats*
> *Benwell once being a village.*

1 mark

3. Award one mark for any answer which conveys a sense of being a prisoner and/or being alone/isolated.

1 mark

4. Award one mark for simple, superficial responses:
> *He likes to go there.*

Award two marks for answers which show an understanding of any one of the following:

> *he went there as a child*
> *could run wild*
> *his body was straight*
> *good times and memories*
> *the trees and wind are the same as when he was a child.*

2 marks

5. This is very much about personal insights and feelings.

Award one mark for simple, superficial responses, e.g.
> *'I feel sorry for him.'*

Award two marks for more developed responses, e.g.
> *'It is sad that he is crippled and has few visitors. I am glad that*
> *he can manage to get to the park and remember his childhood.'*

2 marks

TOTAL 7 marks

PAGE 11 SECTION 4: BOOKLIST

1. Award one mark for each correct answer.

Poetry about the natural world: *Shades of Green*

Information about UFOs: *Newsround book of Space*

Survival in the jungle: *How to Survive in the Jungle*

An amusing view of life in Ancient Egypt: *The Awesome Egyptians*

4 marks

TOTAL 4 marks

IMPROVING YOUR CHILD'S READING AT KS2

- Do talk with your child about what he or she is reading and the way words are used.

- Talk, also, about what YOU are reading.

- Share a range of texts: stories, poems and non-fiction.

- Understanding can be improved by encouraging your child to underline and label important words or sections.

- Encourage your child to list the main points that *he or she* feels are important in a text.

- Let your child devise his or her own questions for a text or section of a text.

- Encourage your child to use a variety of visual representation (e.g. drawings, maps, diagrams) to show characters, setting or information from texts.

- Read together: improve prediction skills by halting the reading at crucial moments so that your child can speculate on what might happen next, using cues from the text.

WRITING TEST ANSWERS

INFORMATION FOR THE PARENT – Writing at KS2: AT3

Effective teaching and learning at KS2 will have taken place when planned from the Programmes of Study for English and implemented in classrooms where talk, reading and writing are integrated. A wide range of evidence about your child as a writer is available to his or her teacher; no test can identify and give a level to the full range of *any* writer's abilities.

The KS2 writing test focuses on several elements from the Programmes of Study. It is designed to gather evidence about a child's ability to:

- construct and convey meaning in written language, matching style to audience and purpose;

- control more complex story forms – attending to structure, detail, setting, character and outcome;

- make meaning clear to the reader and engage the reader's interest;

- use literary stylistic features and be adventurous with vocabulary choices;

- use a wide range of sentence connectives;

- attend to punctuation which demarcates sentences (capital letters, full stops, question marks, exclamation marks);

- set out and punctuate direct speech;

- use commas and paragraphs;

- use written Standard English (except where non-standard or spoken forms are appropriate);

- use pronouns so that things or persons referred to are easily identified;

- use verb tenses in order that shifts in time are consistently and accurately managed;

- ensure agreement between subject and verb within a sentence.

ASSESSING YOUR CHILD'S ANSWER

A full picture of any writer's achievements can only be built up over a period of time in a range of situations. Your child's teacher will have a much fuller view from what has been written during Key Stage 2 than any one-hour test can possibly give. His or her professional skills will provide insight which a parent will be unlikely to match.

The writing test attempts to identify the young writer's achievements in three broad categories:

• Purpose and Organisation
• Grammar
• Style

Few children develop uniformly across these categories.

In marking your child's work, you will be identifying your child's positive achievements as a writer and making judgements about relative strengths and weaknesses in each category. Use the Writing Assessment Criteria table on pages 39–41 to help you to determine your child's score. You will see that your child doesn't need to match all the criteria shown at each level to gain that level. Read the examples of how Cathy's, Sarbjit's and Emily's writing was marked on pages 31–38.

Fill in the box on page 18 with your child's marks.

EXAMPLE ACHIEVEMENTS IN AT3 (WRITING)

Before assessing your child's writing use the Writing Assessment Criteria table (pages 39–41) to identify levels of achievement in writing by three Year 6 pupils, Cathy, Sarbjit and Emily. Start by reading 'Making Friends' by Cathy.

MAKING FRIENDS
written by Cathy Summers
(first draft, with Cathy's own spelling and punctuation)

My name is Cathy Summers. I used to live in Bolton but when I was ten my mum and dad decided to move to Wales because life would be better in the countryside. They put our house up for sale. I was very upset and so were my friends. The day came to move, it was very sad. I was quietly crying and so were my friends. When the family got to Wales we unpacked and I just sat in my new bedroom and cried. My mum came up and tried to comfort me but it didn't work because of the loneliness. About three weeks passed and I never went out not even to school because it was the summer holidays. By now I was fed up. I didn't want to spend my summer hols like this. There was some shops up the road so I decided to ask my Mum for some money so I could go to the shops to buy some sweets. She said 'yes' so off I went. There were some girls and a boy about my age sitting on a wall. They looked bored but friendly. I walked passed to make myself noticed.

3/4 of first page

I looked up for a second and some of them smiled so I smiled back. On my way back from the shops I walked passed the group that were still on the wall. One of them, a thin blonde girl said Hia. What's your name? "Mine is Cathy, what's yours?" I asked. "My name's Adelle, this is Rosylyn, this is Cheryl and this is Philip. You are new here aren't you?" said Adele smiling.

End of first page

I was really happy, I'd made some friends and couldn't wait to tell my Mum. I asked "Any one want a sweet?" "please" they all said together. We all started laughing and I handed the sweets out. Afterwards I hardly had any left but it didn't matter, they were my new friends.

Purpose and Organisation

Refer to the table for Purpose and Organisation on page 39. Begin at Level 3. How does Cathy's story fulfil the criteria?

- There is some description of feelings and motives.
  'I was very upset and so were my friends.'
  '... it was very sad. I was quietly crying ...'
  '... I was really happy ...'
  'I walked passed to make myself noticed.'

- There is detail adding interest.
  '... some of them smiled so I smiled back.'

- Some sensible relation exists between events.
  Events that are connected. Cathy has selected things that are pertinent to her story.

- There is a simple ending relating to the topic.
  'Afterwards I hardly had any left but it didn't matter, they were my new friends.'

Three or more criteria at Level 3 are clearly demonstrated. Cathy is achieving at Level 3. What evidence is there of achievement at Level 4? Look at the criteria for this level. Does Cathy's story meet three or more of these?

- There is a logical relationship between the events of Cathy's story. The relocation leads to loneliness, the trip to the shops to a meeting with new friends, the new friends lead to happiness. There is some paragraphing.

- There is some characterisation and there is significant interaction – between Cathy and her old friends, Cathy and her mother and Cathy and her new friends.

- Description is used to develop characterisation.
  Her mother's actions convey kindness.
  'They looked bored but friendly.'
  The laughter conveys happiness.

- Given the limitations of time, Cathy has paced her story. It is detailed, there is a clear beginning, middle and end.

- Awareness of the reader is shown through comments about events and characters.
  '... life would be better in the countryside ...'
  '... they were my new friends.'
  '... because it was the summer holidays.'

Cathy has clearly demonstrated achievement against three or more criteria at Level 4. Is there evidence of any achievements at Level 5?

- There is evidence of competence in using story conventions but *not* of flexibility.

- The central plot is convincing.

- Although dialogue, action and description are used, these are not developed.

• Indications of thoughts and feelings are limited – there is no development of viewpoint or narrative.

• Paragraphing is not consistent.

Although this story shows some evidence of achievement at Level 5 it is insufficient for that level to be given. It does meet sufficient criteria at Level 4 (Purpose and Organisation), therefore award 8 marks.

Grammar

Next refer to the table for Grammar on page 40 and see how Cathy's story meets the criteria. Begin at Level 3.

• At least half of the sentences on the first page are correctly punctuated with capital letters and full stops or question marks. Cathy has clearly achieved Level 3.

Now compare the grammar of her story with the criteria for Level 4.

• At least 3/4 of the sentences are correctly punctuated using capital letters followed by full stops, question marks or exclamation marks.

• Commas are used to separate items on a list.
  '... this is Rosylyn, this is Cheryl, this is Philip.'

• Speech punctuation is generally accurate.

• The use of pronouns is inconsistent but pronouns are used.

Cathy has clearly demonstrated achievement against two or more criteria at Level 4. Is there evidence of any achievements at Level 5?

• There are more than two lapses in punctuation.
  'please' (capital letter missing)
  Hia. What's your name (speech marks and question mark missing)

• Tenses and pronouns used consistently.

Cathy does not meet both criteria for Level 5 (Grammar). She has met sufficient criteria for Level 4, therefore award 4 marks.

Style

Now refer to the table for Style on page 41 and identify Cathy's achievements, beginning at Level 3.

• There is use of connectives.
  'because', 'when', 'but', 'by', 'now'

• There are simple noun phrases.
  'my new bedroom', 'a blond girl'

One or more criteria for style are met: Level 3 is achieved for Style. Now identify achievements for Level 4.

• There is a preponderance of written language structures. Cathy informs us of her name and situation, avoids repetition and summarises when necessary. She uses the literary convention of resolution at the end of her story.

• Subordinating connectives are used.
  'By now...', 'because of...'

• There is use of expansion before or after the subject noun.
  '... about my age, sitting on a wall'
  '... not even to school'

Two or more criteria at Level 4 are met. Are there achievements at Level 5?

• The story is in written in Standard English and she uses dialect (slang *'Hia'*) when appropriate.

• She does not differentiate speech from writing using complex sentence structures.

• Vocabulary is not particularly varied and interesting.

Cathy does not meet two or more criteria Level 5 (Style). Her story does meet sufficient criteria for Level 4 (Style) so 4 marks are awarded and Cathy's writing test score looks like this:

	Cathy's Writing Test Score
Purpose and Organisation	8
Grammar	4
Style	4
WRITING TEST TOTAL	16

Now consider a second story, 'Future Life' by Sarbjit.

FUTURE LIFE
by Sarbjit Kapoor
(first draft, with Sarbjit's own spelling and punctuation)

The year is 2050 A.D.
The date 20/11/50
The place Oldham, Lands End (due to raised sea-level due to global warming), England.

My Grandad, Sarbjit Kapoor, had first told me about his Ford XR3 convertible when I was ten in 2044. It had been his first car, he'd bought it in 2002 A.D. He told me how he'd saved and saved to buy it after he passed his driving test. The car was already ten years old then. 'The best car in the universe' he claimed. 'Is there such a thing,' I'd asked 'I'd settle for the worst car in the world. I'd settle for any car at all!' 'Well when you are sixteen I'll take you out for a drive, but don't tell your Mum,' he whispered.

The sun rose early – a green dawn like flourescent gas. The atmosphere had never been clear since the war between Japan and the U.S.A.
'I've managed to get some petrol my old friend Darren had.'
'Great Grandad, the roboid cars now are all electric or gas.'
'I'll drive us out to the old motorway across the moors – the M62, I know a secret way onto a smooth bit.'
'We'll after look out for Police Capsules.'

It was my sixteenth birthday – the time had come for my first drive in A MOTORCAR! My name is Zeeko Kapoor. I live in an underground house near Oldham, overlooking the sea. 9/10th of the world is now ocean because of global warming. I live with my family and my Grandad.
*   My heart was beating like a hammer with excitement. Would he let me have a drive, I wondered. I'd never been in a real car before.*
*   Grandad turned the ignition key. The engine coughed and spluttered, the car jumped forward. Soon we were doing fifty miles an hour, the wind rushing through my hair, my eyes were stung by it.*
*   It was really great, cars now were all Roboids, very safe but VERY boring. The old car was a bit rattly even though Grandad had looked after it carefully.*

'FASTER' I shouted, we were now doing 90 m.p.h. Suddenly he slammed the brakes on.
'Look out,' I screamed.
After that everything went black.
I awoke to find my parents gathered around my bed.
'How's Grandad?' I asked.
'He's O.K.' said Dad.
'What happened?'
'You hit a sheep, Grandad swerved and you left the motoway.'
'It's all my fault, I wanted him to go faster.'
'Don't worry son, Grandad hasn't enjoyed himself so much since he won the British Grand Prix in 2010 A.D.' laughed Dad.

Later that day Granded was moved into the same ward.
'I've got some great news,' he told me, 'We're being sent to the space hospital to recover! They say the lack of gravity gets you better quicker.'
'That was a great drive, you can see why cars are banned.'
'Yes, but it's a pity the car was smashed up.' It had been a great day.

Purpose and Organisation

Refer to the table for Purpose and Organisation on page 39 to consider whether Sarbjit's story meets the criteria for Level 4.

- The events do relate. There is paragraphing.

- Characters are developed, they *do* interact.
  'It was my sixteenth birthday.'

- Development within the action conveys character.
  'The best car in the universe' he claimed.
  'Is there such a thing,' I'd asked.

- The story is paced and detailed, with a beginning, middle and end.

- Comments show awareness of the reader.
  'I live with my family and my Grandad ...'

Three or more criteria are clearly demonstrated: Level 4 is achieved. Is there achievement at Level 5 – does Sarbjit meet three or more of these criteria?

- Use of story conventions is competent and flexible.
  He opens the main action half way through the circumstances (*'My Grandad, Sarbjit Kapoor, had first ...'*)
  There is use of snatches of dialogue.
  'The best car in the world ...'
  '... don't tell your Mum,' he whispered.
  There is synopsis.
  'It had been his first car, he'd bought it in 2002 A.D.'

- The plot and ending are convincing.

- The point of view and narrative voice are developed.
  'Would he let me have a drive, I wondered?'
  'It was really great, cars now were all Roboids, very safe but VERY boring.'
  'It had been a great day.'

• Paragraphs do consistently mark major episodes.

Certainly three or more criteria for Purpose and Organisation are met. Sarbjit's story is definitely Level 5. Is there evidence of achievements at Level 6?

• Within the limits of this task we see themes (technological change, environmental change) developed.

• There are a number of linked episodes.

• There is some reflection on characters and actions, the story moves backwards and forwards in time, suspense or surprise is less marked.

• Paragraphing ensures coherent organisation.

• Spoken dialogue is clearly laid out.

Three or more criteria for Level 6 (Purpose and Organisation) are met. Award 12 marks.

Grammar

Now refer to the table for Grammar on page 40. Compare Sarbjit's criteria with the criteria for Level 3. The criteria are met. The same is true of Levels 4 and 5. Both criteria at Level 6 are met. Therefore award 6 marks.

Style

Now refer to the table for Style on page 41 and identify Sarbjit's achievements, beginning at Level 4.

• Written language structures are used.

• Subordinating connectives are used.
  'Suddenly,' 'After that...'

• Expansion is used before or after subject nouns.
  'the worst car in the world.'
  'the old motorway across the moors.'

Two or more criteria for Level 4 (Style) are met. Now compare the story to the criteria for Level 5.

• There is no choice of dialect in the story. Sarbjit has chosen to use Standard English throughout, therefore that criteria is met.

• Speech and writing are differentiated. Sarbjit uses the passive voice.
  'The sun rose early –' The subject of the sentence (the sun) is the 'goal' of the action.
  'My eyes were stung by it.' The subject of the phrase (my eyes) is the goal of the action.

He also avoids repetition, referring backwards and forwards to subject matter.

• Varied and interesting vocabulary are recognised.
  'a green dawn like flourescent gas.'
  'My heart was beating like a hammer'

Sarbjit has met two or more criteria for Level 5 (Style).

It is now worth comparing the story with the criteria for Level 6.

- Noun phrases are expanded and elaborated.
  'a green dawn like flourescent gas.'
  'overlooking the sea.'
  'the wind rushing through my hair...'

- There is a varied choice of verbs.
  'claimed', 'asked', 'whispered'

- The order of words and phrases within sentences is chosen to develop themes and sustain interest.
  'a green dawn like flourescent gas.'
  'The time had come for my first drive in A MOTOR CAR!'

- Deliberate patterning for emphasis and rhythm does not appear to be present in Sarbjit's story.

- Sarbjit has not chosen to use dialect for characterisation.

Sarbjit meets three or more criteria at Level 6. Six marks should be awarded and his Writing Test Score looks like this:

	Sarbjit's Writing Test Score
Purpose and Organisation	12
Grammar	6
Style	6
WRITING TEST TOTAL	24

When setting a level for your child's story, remember that only a number of the criteria need to be met for that level to be awarded as stated in the Writing Assessment Criteria table on pages 39–41.

Given the limitations of this test do be positive in your review of the evidence. Sarbjit's story is particularly full of evidence: quite small examples are sufficient for the criteria to be met.

Now consider a piece of descriptive writing, 'My Grandad Drever' by Emily.

MY GRANDAD DREVER
by Emily Drever
(first draft, with Emily's own spelling and punctuation)

My Grandad Drever lives on his own in a bungalow near Cheddleton. He has lived there since he retired. He used to have his own business as a plumber.

He is a very kind man and laughs a lot. He is 69 years old and has been on his own since my Nan died in 1992. He loves his garden. It is always very tidy and full of flowers. He grows beautiful roses.

Every Sunday Grandad Drever visits us for his tea. He always brings me a present, sometimes chocolate or sweets, sometimes something interesting he has bought at a car-boot. Last week he got me a coral necklace. It is nice of him to get me things but I don't always like them. I pretend I do!

He likes car-boot sales. He buys old brass and shines it up and sells it. He also makes bird houses and bird tables and sells them.

3/4 of first page

I think he misses my Nan a lot. He likes to show me photographs of them when they were young.

He is a fit man. He walks his dog, Megan, every day down by the canal. He is tall and has white hair. He eyes are blue and his skin is very tanned.

End of first page

There are little lines on his face. He does not watch much television, except travel programmes. He likes wildlife and different parts of the world. My Grandad is a good friend to me, I love him very much.

Purpose and Organisation

Refer to the table for Purpose and Organisation on page 39. Elements of Level 4 are clearly shown.

- There is some logic to the structure and paragraphs are used. Character is developed by description as is setting.
  'full of flowers'

- Comments develop this description.
  '... I don't always like them.'
  '... he misses my Nan a lot.'

- The description is paced and detailed and Emily shows awareness of the reader through comments.
  '... I don't always like them.'
  'My Grandad is a good friend to me... '

Three or more criteria for Level 4 are clearly demonstrated. It's now necessary to check for achievements at Level 5; does the writer meet three or more of these?

- Description is developed.
  '... he grows beautiful roses.'
  '... he is tall and has white hair. His eyes are blue and his skin is very tanned. There are little lines on his face.'

- Narrative voice is also developed.
  '... I pretend I do!'
  'I think he misses my Nan a lot.'

- Paragraph divisions consistently mark major episodes of the writing.

Emily has met three criteria at Level 5. A review of criteria for Level 6 shows that she fails to meet sufficient criteria, therefore she is awarded ten marks.

Grammar

Next refer to the table for Grammar on page 40. This shows that Emily has achieved enough criteria to fufil Level 6. Award 6 marks.

Style

Now consider Emily's story against the criteria for Style on page 41.

- At Level 4 written language structures are used, repetition is avoided and there is summary.
  '... he always brings me something interesting.'

- Subordinating connectives give meaning.
  '... but I don't always like them.'
  'He also makes bird houses... '

Emily gains Level 4 for Style. Does she meet Level 5? Standard English is quite appropriately used, as are written language constructions. Vocabulary is generally varied and interesting. This is sufficient for Level 5.

Next check the writing against Level 6 for Style.

- Noun phrases are expanded and elaborated.
  'He is a very kind man and laughs a lot.'
  'He likes to show me photographs of them when they were young.'

- There is little variation in verbs or abverbs. 'Enjoyed', 'appreciate', 'loves', would make effective alternatives to the much-used 'like'. 'Very' is also over-used.

- There is some attempt to vary the order of phrases. 'Last week...' and 'Every Sunday...' make a change from beginning sentences 'He... ' or 'My Grandad... '.

Emily is able to pattern for emphasis and rhythm.
'... sometimes chocolate or sweets, sometimes something interesting... '
'I pretend I do! I love him very much.'

She has met three or more criteria for Style. Award 6 marks.

	Emily's Writing Test Score
Purpose and Organisation	10
Grammar	6
Style	6
WRITING TEST TOTAL	22

WRITING ASSESSMENT CRITERIA

1.	PURPOSE AND ORGANISATION	Maximum 12 marks

LEVEL 3

As a whole the writing shows:

- some detail in the description of setting or characters' feelings or motives
- details adding interest or humour or suspense
- some sensible relation between events or ideas (i.e. selected highlights from chronological sequence, not every happening)
- a simple ending relating to topic.

Award 6 marks if two or more criteria (•) are met.

LEVEL 4

- ideas or events in the writing relate to each other with some logicality and some paragraphing
- story 'characters' developed for the purpose of the story, some significant interaction between them or personality of central figure developed
- characterisation developed within the writing (e.g. by use of direct or reported speech or by description)
- length of writing well judged with respect to pacing and detail; beginning, middle and end suitably distinguished
- comments on characters or events show awareness of reader (these may be quite brief).

Award 8 marks if three or more criteria (•) are met.

LEVEL 5

- competent and flexible use of story or descriptive conventions, e.g. ability to experiment with story opening – starting in the middle of circumstances, or with snatches of dialogue, or with narrator's synopsis
- convincing central plot or character and ending or conclusion
- ability to develop elements of dialogue, action, description where appropriate
- development of point of view and 'narrative voice' (e.g. asides to reader, comments on action, indication of character's thoughts and feelings)
- paragraph divisions mark major episodes of story (e.g. beginning, start of action and/or final resolution), different aspects of central character described.

Award 10 marks if three or more criteria (•) are met.

LEVEL 6

- development of theme (e.g. loneliness, friendship) or personality (e.g. humour, kindness) as well as plot (the happenings of the story) or, in a descriptive piece, the attitudes or values of the person
- contains a number of linked episodes or sections
- reflections on characters and actions and, if appropriate, non-linear time line, management of suspense or surprise
- use of paragraphs to ensure coherent organisation
- any spoken dialogue is clearly laid out.

Award 12 marks if three or more criteria (•) are met.

2.	GRAMMAR	Maximum 6 marks

L E V E L 3

Assess on the first full page:

• at least half the sentences are correctly punctuated using capital letters and full stops or question marks.

Award 3 marks if this criteria (•) is met.

L E V E L 4

Assess on first full page:

• at least three-quarters of the sentences are correctly punctuated using capital letters followed by full stops, question marks or exclamation marks
• developing use of comma to separate phrases or clauses in sequence, items on list
• speech punctuation generally accurate
• consistent use of tenses and pronouns.

Award 4 marks if two or more criteria (•) are met.

L E V E L 5

Assess on first full page:

• no more than two lapses in punctuation of sentences, or in direct speech
• consistent and appropriate use of tenses and pronouns.

Award 5 marks if both criteria (•) are met.

L E V E L 6

Assess on complete text:

• sustained accurate use of punctuation (see above), tenses, pronouns
• evidence of decisions to vary sentence length for clarity and change of narrative pace.

Award 6 marks if both criteria (•) are met.

3.	STYLE	Maximum 6 marks

LEVEL 3

Assess on the writing as a whole:

- evidence of beginning to shape writing by use of a wider range of connectives (*'but'*, *'when'*, *'so'*, *'because'*, etc.) to indicate relation between ideas (e.g. *'contrast'*, *'connection in time'*, *'explanation'*)

Award 3 marks

LEVEL 4

- greater use of written language structures, e.g. avoids repetition
- use of subordinating connectives to give meaning, e.g. *'as if'*, *'instead'*, *'so that'*, *'because of'*
- beginning of use of expansion before or after the subject noun for description and comment, e.g. *'battered Land Rover'*, *'a goat with bad breath'*.

Award 4 marks if two or more criteria (•) are met.

LEVEL 5

- appropriate choice between Standard English and dialect
- differentiation of speech from writing:

  e.g. use of written language constructions, such as passive voice, to alter focus of attention

  e.g. use of constructions to avoid repetition, such as grouping of several subjects before a main verb, referring back/forward to subject matter.
- greater use of varied and interesting vocabulary.

Award 5 marks if two or more criteria (•) are met.

LEVEL 6

- expansion and elaboration of noun phrases to enhance description of characters and feelings
- varied choice of verbs (*'screamed'*, *'begged'*), and adverbs (*'two reasonably well behaved children'*) gives shades of meaning
- within sentences, order of words and phrases chosen to develop themes of story and sustain reader interest
- deliberate patterning for emphasis and rhythm (*'Thunder sounded, lightning flashed and hard rain began to pour'*)
- use of dialect, if needed, for characterisation.

Award 6 marks if three or more criteria (•) are met.

IMPROVING YOUR CHILD'S WRITING AT KS2

- Plan and draft writing.

- Use paragraphs: ideas which go together in separate sections, starting on a new line.

- Use some spoken dialogue, set down correctly using speech marks and a new line for each person speaking.

- Punctuate correctly.

- Use tenses and pronouns correctly.

- Use varied, interesting vocabulary.

- Use descriptive language to convey settings, characters and feelings.

CAPITAL LETTERS
Remind your child of the purpose of capital letters.

1. As the first letter of a sentence
   He went on walking.

2. For the personal pronoun 'I'
   I did not hurt her.

3. At the beginning of a new piece of direct speech
   Leo shouted, "Come on, you crazy goat."

4. For the first letter of a proper noun
   People's names: *Gillian Cross*
   Places: *High Street, Coventry, England*
   Titles of books, plays, films, TV programmes: *Rescuing Gloria, Horizon*
   Days of the week: *Wednesday*
   Brand names: *Land Rover*
   Months of the year: *August*
   Planets and stars: *Venus*

5. For the first letter of titles of people and organisations
   The Prince of Wales
   Royal Society for the Protection of Birds

6. For the initials in the names of people and organisations
   Edward G. Robinson
   Liverpool F.C.

7. For initials used in abbreviations
   BBC, RSPCA

FULL STOPS, QUESTIONS MARKS AND EXCLAMATION MARKS
Normal sentences must end with one of these three marks:

.	?	!
full stop	question mark	exclamation mark

Statements normally end with a **full stop**.
There was a goat in the back.

A **question** normally ends with a **question mark**.
What can I do?

Exclamation marks are used to mark an **exclamation**, or **forceful statement**.
But that's six weeks!

COMMAS
Commas help a reader pass over the page of print. They make sentences easier to read and understand. They are used to:

1. Separate the items in a list
   At Christmas they bought me a Christmas tree, decorations, mince pies, and a present.

2. Separate the clauses in a sentence
   Gloria the goat turned towards him, snuffling her nose into his hand as he got close.

3. Mark off phrases that are separate from the main part of the sentence.
   They were standing by a lamp-post, about a hundred yards away, chatting and kicking a football about.

WRITING DOWN DIRECT SPEECH
1. Every piece of speech is enclosed between double or single inverted commas. In books single inverted commas are normally used. In school your child may have been taught to use double inverted commas.

2. Every new piece of speech must begin with a capital letter, even if it is not the first word in the sentence.

3. Each piece of speech must end with a full stop or an exclamation mark or a question mark before the concluding inverted commas...

4. ... unless the sentence is going to continue, when it ends with a comma. This also comes before the concluding inverted commas.

5. For each new speaker you start a new line and indent.

   'I wasn't hurting her,' Leo said quickly. 'Only talking to her.'
   'I can tell that, boy. She likes you.' The old man took a chunk of cabbage out of his pocket. 'Give her this.'
   Rather nervously, Leo took the cabbage and held it out. Gloria lunged forward to take a bite.
   'That's it, girl,' the old man said. His voice crackled strangely. 'You have some fun while you can. You've only got another ten minutes or so.'
   Leo looked at Gloria as she chewed. 'Why only ten minutes? What's going to happen then?'

NOTES

Use this space to make notes about the achievements you have identified in your child's piece of writing.

IMPROVING YOUR CHILD'S SPELLING AT KS2

PATTERNS
English spelling is not chaotic. Three-quarters of all words follow regular patterns. Encourage your child to be aware of patterns of letters used to spell particular sounds.

WORD FAMILIES
Encourage your child to look for word families.
author, authorise, authority, authorisation

In this family of four words *author* is spelled the same. *-ity, -ise, -isation* are spelled in the same way. Looking for families like this makes spelling easier.

A WAY TO LEARN SPELLINGS
1. **LOOK** at the correct spelling of the word and say it. It could help you to write it out five times.

2. **COVER** the word and **REMEMBER** it.

3. **WRITE** it from memory.

4. **CHECK** it with the original.

5. If it's wrong, repeat stages 1–4.

MAKING PLURALS
Plural means 'more than one'. Most words follow rules. For example:

1. Normally, just add -**s**.
*book – book**s**.*

2. Words that end in -**s**, add -**es**.
*glass – glass**es***

3. Words that end in -**x** and -**z**, add -**es.**
*fox – fox**es***

4. Words that end in -**ch** and -**sh**, add -**es.**
*branch – branch**es***

5. Words that end in -**f** or -**fe** change the ending to -**ve** and add -**s**.
Exceptions: *belie**fs**, chie**fs**, dwar**fs**, grie**fs**, gul**fs**, proo**fs**, roo**fs***

6. Words that end in -**y**, if the letter before the **y** is a vowel just add -**s**.
*day – day**s***

If the letter before the **y** is a consonant change the -**y** to -**ies**.
*baby – bab**ies***

7. Words that end in -**o** usually just need an -**s**.
*piano – piano**s***
Exceptions: *volcano**es**, hero**es**, tomato**es**, go**es**, potato**es***

8. Some words stay the same in the plural.
aircraft, sheep, deer

9. Some words change in a different way.
child – children
mouse – mice
woman – women

10. Some Latin and Greek words change in different ways.
crisis – crises
formula – formulae

ADDING -ING AND -ED
Verbs change according to the sentence they are in.
I <u>walk</u> to school. I <u>walked</u> to school yesterday and I am <u>walking</u> to school now.

1. Normally you just add -**ing** or -**ed**.

There are some exceptions. The main ones are:

hop<u>e</u> – hop<u>ing</u>	cr<u>y</u> – cr<u>ied</u>
smok<u>e</u> – smok<u>ing</u>	tr<u>y</u> – tr<u>ied</u>
sto<u>p</u> – sto<u>pping</u>	sto<u>p</u> – sto<u>pped</u>
ru<u>n</u> – ru<u>nning</u>	

2. Word with one syllable, with a long vowel, ending in -<u>e</u>. Remove the -<u>e</u> and add -<u>ed</u> and -<u>ing</u>.
dare, dar<u>ed</u>, dar<u>ing</u>

3. Words with one syllable, with a short vowel, ending in a single consonant. Double the consonant and add -<u>ed</u> and -<u>ing</u>.
beg, beg<u>ged</u>, beg<u>ging</u>

4. Words with more than one syllable, ending in a single consonant. If the last syllable is stressed, double the consonant.
propel, propel<u>led</u>, propel<u>ling</u>

If the stress is not on the last syllable, just add -<u>ed</u> and -<u>ing.</u>
sharpen, sharpen<u>ed</u>, sharpen<u>ing</u>

5. Words ending in -<u>l</u>. If there is only a single vowel before the -<u>l</u>, just add -<u>ed</u> and -<u>ing</u>.
peel, peel<u>ed</u>, peel<u>ing</u>

6. Words ending in -<u>y</u>.
If the letter before the -<u>y</u> is a vowel, just add -<u>ed</u> and -<u>ing</u>.
stay, stay<u>ed</u>, stay<u>ing</u>
Exceptions: *lay – laid, say – said, pay – paid*

If the letter before the -<u>y</u> is a consonant change the -<u>y</u> to an -<u>i</u> before adding -<u>ed</u>.
fry, fr<u>ied</u>, fry<u>ing</u>

ADDING -LY
Turn adjectives into adverbs by adding -<u>ly</u>.
He is a slow driver. He drives slow<u>ly</u>.

Usually you just add -<u>ly</u> to the adjective.

Exceptions:
1. If the word ends -<u>ll</u> just add -<u>y</u>.
full – ful<u>ly</u>

2. If a word of two or more syllables ends in -<u>y</u> cut off the -<u>y</u> add -<u>ily</u>.
happy – happ<u>ily</u>

3. One-syllable words ending in -<u>y</u> are usually regular.
shy – shy<u>ly</u>
Exception: *day – daily*

4. If the words end in -<u>le</u> cut off the -<u>e</u> and add -<u>y</u>.
simple – simp<u>ly</u>.

READING BOOKS
Reading will not make everyone a perfect speller but it is difficult to be really good at spelling if you read nothing at all.

ASSESSING YOUR CHILD'S HANDWRITING

Compare your child's copy of the handwriting passage with these examples and decide which best matches their achievements.

Accurately formed letters, consistent in size.   2 marks

> Who could say how successful their journey
> might be?
> Could this brave mission find a place for
> the human race somewhere deep in space?

Handwriting *begins* to be joined and is legible.   3 marks

> Who could say how successful their
> Journey might be?
> Could this brave mission, find a
> place for the human race?

More fluent, joined and legible handwriting.   4 marks

> Who could say how successful their journey might
> be? Could this brave mission find a place for
> the human race somewhere deep in space?

Joined, clear and fluent handwriting.   5 marks

> Who could say how successful their journey might be?
> Could this brave mission find a place for the human
> race, somewhere deep in space?

Handwriting is consistently fluent and legible, clear and attractive.   6 marks

> Who could say how successful their journey might be?
> Could this brave mission find a place for the human race,
> somewhere deep in space?

Total 6 marks

IMPROVING YOUR CHILD'S HANDWRITING AT KS2

Fluency and clarity may be improved by attending to these points:

• Sit in a relaxed, comfortable way, not too close to the table.

• Hold the pen so that there is control and comfort, avoiding tension and too tight a grip.

• Start all letters at the top except **d** and **e**.

• Make letters neither too large nor too small.

• All similar letters should be the same height.

• Strokes above (**b, d, f, h, k, l, t**) and below (**g, j, p, q, y**) should be clearly visible.

FINDING YOUR CHILD'S LEVEL FOR ENGLISH

There are four stages to finding the overall English test level.

1. Note your child's Reading Test Total from page 11.

	Reading Test Total

2. Note your child's Writing Test Total from page 18.

	Writing Test Total

3. Use the table below to convert your child's Spelling Score from page 21 and your child's Handwriting Score from page 21 to find the Presentation Mark.

18	Spelling Score

6	Handwriting Score

Handwriting Score

Spelling Score	2	3	4	5	6
0	**1**	1	1	2	2
1–4	**2**	2	3	3	3
5–7	**3**	3	3	4	4
8–13	**3**	4	4	4	5
14–18	**4**	5	5	5	(6)
19–20	**5**	5	6	6	6

Read down from the column which contains your child's Handwriting Score and read across from the row giving your child's Spelling Score.

This Presentation Mark should be between 0 and 6.

6	Presentation Mark *(Spelling and Handwriting)*

Add the Presentation Mark and the Writing Test Total mark together. This gives the Writing Total Mark, between 0 and 30.

	Writing Total Mark *(Presentation Mark plus Writing Test Total)*

4. Now use the table below to find the English test level.

Reading Test Total

Writing Total Mark (Presentation Mark plus Writing Test Total)	0–2	3–10	11–25	26–43	44–54	55–61
0–2	*	2	2	3	4	4
3–6	1	2	3	3	4	5
7–11	2	2	3	4	4	5
12–16	2	3	3	4	5	5
17–21	3	3	4	4	5	6
22–26	3	4	4	(5)	5	6
27–30	4	4	5	5	6	6

Read down from the column which contains your child's Reading Test Total and read across from the row giving your child's Writing Total Mark.

The Key Stage 2 test level is the number shown where the row for Writing and the column for Reading intersect.

	KS2 English level *(Reading Test Total and Writing Total Mark)*

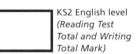

EXAMPLE
In the reading test Abigail scores 29.

In the writing test she scores 14 marks (8 for Purpose and Organisation, 3 for Grammar and 3 for Style).

She scores 11 marks in the Spelling Test and 4 marks for Handwriting, giving a Presentation Mark of 4 from the conversion table.

Adding her Presentation Mark (4) and her Writing Test Score (14) together gives a Writing Total Mark of 18.

The English test level table shows that Abigail's reading score is in the column headed 26–43. The Writing Total Mark is in the range 17–21, so the overall Key Stage 2 English test level is 4.

PASSAGE TO READ ALOUD

NOTE TO PARENT

Detatch this page so you can read this passage aloud while your child does the spelling test on pages 20–21.

Through Space in 'Eternity'

All around the Earth people **looked** on as the **time** rapidly **approached** for the launch of United Nations' deep space craft *Eternity*.

Their minds were **concentrating** on a billion virtual **reality** sets. The **power** of many lasers **illuminated** the launch site, cutting the African night; tension was mounting inside the **command** centre. The plan was to explore space in the remote control craft, seeking some **planet** on which human life could be established.

Why was this voyage taking place? By the year 2050 A.D. Earth had become even more crowded. The population multiplied and consumed at an ever-increasing rate. Human selfishness had destroyed **nature**, now humanity itself was threatened. It **appeared** that nothing could prevent an environmental disaster.

The **capacity** of the deep space craft was limited. From a million volunteers from all over the **world** only one hundred were chosen. Life on a new planet would be difficult. Tolerance, intelligence and **confidence** were particularly important qualities.

The journey they faced was long. Medical science knew how to **freeze** them, injections of **gold** would stop bones from **crumbling**, artificial **material** replaced blood.

Many dangers lay ahead. Barring **accidents**, the travellers would reach their destination in 2150 A.D., having **slept** for a century!

PAGE 20–21 SPELLING TEST

1.	looked	1 mark
2.	time	1 mark
3.	approached	1 mark
4.	concentrating –	1 mark
5.	reality –	1 mark
6.	power	1 mark
7.	illuminated	1 mark
8.	command	1 mark
9.	planet	1 mark
10.	nature	1 mark
11.	appeared	1 mark
12.	capacity	1 mark
13.	world	1 mark
14.	confidence	1 mark
15.	freeze	1 mark
16.	gold	1 mark
17.	crumbling	1 mark
18.	material	1 mark
19.	accidents	1 mark
20.	slept	1 mark

Total 20 marks

SPELLING AND HANDWRITING TEST ANSWERS

INFORMATION FOR THE PARENT – Spelling and Handwriting at KS2: ATs 4,4/5

During the course of Key Stage 2 children have been enabled to develop their individual ability in recognising, knowing and applying:

• single syllable words which follow common patterns
  cold, sold, gold

• regularly used multi-syllable words
  because, animal, together, planet

• common regular vowel patterns and letter strings
  slave, cave, grave; –ing, –ion, –ous

• word families and their relationships
  freeze, freezing, frozen; sleep, sleeping, slept

• more complex words
  crumble, crumbling, crumbled; accident, accidental

• words with related meaning which have related spellings, even though they sound different
  sign, signature; medical, medicine; manage, managerial

• *They have also developed their ability to produce handwriting which is joined, fluent, legible, clear and attractive.*